Jimmy Carter

History Maker Bios

Laura Hamilton Waxman

BARNES & NOBLE

NEW YORK

TABLE OF CONTENTS

INTRODUCTION 5

1. "HOTSHOT" 6

2. FROM OFFICER TO BUSINESSMAN 14

3. LEADER IN GEORGIA 21

4. PRESIDENT CARTER 27

5. PEACEMAKER 37

TIMELINE 44

ROSALYNN CARTER:
A GREAT AMERICAN WOMAN 45

FURTHER READING 46

WEBSITES 46

SELECT BIBLIOGRAPHY 47

INDEX 48

Introduction

Jimmy Carter grew up on a big farm in Georgia. His parents taught him to work hard. They taught him to be fair and honest. And they taught him to always look for new challenges.

Carter became president of the United States in 1977. Right away, he set himself to many tough challenges. In all his work, he tried to be as honest and fair as he could.

He found a new challenge after his four years as president. In the 1980s, he opened the Carter Center. The Carter Center tries to bring peace to countries at war. It also helps people in need. Jimmy Carter has inspired many people with his hard work for his country and the world.

This is his story.

1 "HOTSHOT"

J ames Earl Carter Jr. was born in Plains, Georgia, on the morning of October 1, 1924. He was the first child of Lillian and James Earl Carter. They called him Jimmy.

When Jimmy was three years old, his family moved to a nearby town called Archery. There Jimmy grew up with two younger sisters, Gloria and Ruth. He also had a baby brother named Billy.

The family lived in a simple wooden farmhouse. They used firewood to cook and heat their home. For many years, they had no electricity or running water.

Jimmy's father, known as Earl, ran a large farm and business. Peanuts and cotton were the main crops on the Carter farm. Earl also grew other crops, such as potatoes, corn, and watermelons. He raised pigs, cows, sheep, and other animals.

Jimmy stands with his father, Earl, and his sisters Gloria (FAR LEFT) and Ruth (CENTER) outside their farmhouse in Archery, Georgia.

Jimmy looked up to his father as a hero. Earl rose before sunrise each morning. He began working right after breakfast. And he didn't stop working until dark. It took every minute of the day to get everything done.

Jimmy wanted to work hard too. He learned to boil, bag, and sell peanuts by the time he was six years old. His father taught him to save the money he earned.

As Jimmy grew older, he took on other chores. His father called Jimmy "hotshot." He always gave Jimmy new challenges.

Jimmy rides Lady and leads the colt, Lady Lee. The family dog, Sam, follows close behind them.

Lillian Carter holds her son Jimmy.

Jimmy's mother also worked hard. Lillian was a nurse in the nearby hospital. She helped sick people in their homes too. She didn't care if a sick person was black or white. That was unusual in the South at that time. Many white southerners did not treat black people with respect. They would never enter a black person's home. Lillian taught Jimmy to treat everyone, black or white, with respect and kindness.

Jimmy (TOP LEFT), Gloria (BOTTOM LEFT), and Ruth (BOTTOM RIGHT) enjoy the company of friends.

Most of Jimmy's neighbors were black sharecroppers. Sharecroppers rented homes and land from a farmer. Some sharecroppers paid the farmer with the crops they grew. Others paid with money they earned from selling crops. It was a hard life. Most of the black families Jimmy knew lived in small shacks. They barely had enough money and food to get by.

Jimmy was friendly with the children in these families. Like Jimmy, they worked hard on Earl's farm. They also had some time for fun. Jimmy and his friends fished, hunted, climbed trees, and played sports.

But segregation laws in the South kept Jimmy and his friends apart in other ways. These laws said that black people and white people should live separately. Jimmy's church was for white people only. His school was the same way. Some of his friends attended churches and schools that were for black people only.

SEGREGATION

Segregation harmed African Americans all over the South. Black citizens were not allowed to enter restaurants or movie theaters that were reserved for whites only. They had to use separate bathrooms and drinking fountains. Schools for white children were much nicer than schools for black children. And black children had to walk to school. White children, such as Jimmy, rode the bus.

Jimmy worked as hard at school as he did on the farm. He needed good grades to make his dream come true. Jimmy wanted to be the first person in his family to go to college. He planned to go to the United States Naval Academy in Annapolis, Maryland. Then he would join the navy like his Uncle Tom Gordy. Uncle Gordy sent Jimmy postcards from different parts of the world. The postcards made navy life seem exciting.

Jimmy (FIRST ROW, FAR RIGHT) graduated from Plains High School in 1941.

Rosalynn Smith was also born in Plains, Georgia.

In 1941, Jimmy graduated from Plains High School at the top of his class. He went to college in Georgia for two years. Then he was accepted to the United States Naval Academy in Annapolis. He lived and studied at the academy for most of the year. He went back to Georgia during the summers.

One of those summers, Jimmy met the best friend of his sister Ruth. Her name was Rosalynn Smith. Rosalynn was smart and interesting. Jimmy asked her out on a date. That very same night, Jimmy made a decision. One day, he would marry Rosalynn Smith.

2 FROM OFFICER TO BUSINESSMAN

Carter graduated from the U.S. Naval Academy in June 1946. He married Rosalynn one month later. The next year they had their first child, John. They called him Jack. Rosalynn stayed at home with Jack while her husband was away at sea.

Carter liked being an officer in the navy. He worked as hard as ever. That way, the navy would give him new challenges. His hard work paid off. In 1949, the navy made Carter an officer on a submarine. The navy chose only the best officers to work on these underwater ships. Carter's submarine was near Honolulu, Hawaii, so Rosalynn and Jack moved there.

A Hardworking Officer

Carter spent weeks away from Honolulu on the navy submarine. Those days were filled with nonstop work. After dinner, other officers talked, laughed, and played card games. Not Carter. He always found more things to do. In the evenings, he read books or made repairs on the submarine.

Carter spent his free time at home with his wife and son. The Carters loved life in Hawaii. They explored the beaches and made new friends. Rosalynn also gave birth to their second son, James Earl III. They called him Chip.

Carter worked on other submarines in other parts of the country. Then the navy gave him another new challenge. In 1952, the navy asked him to be a top officer on one of the first nuclear submarines. Being chosen for the job was a great honor.

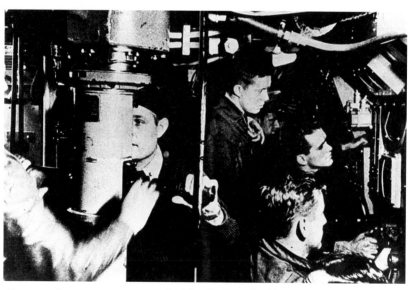

Carter (STANDING CENTER) liked the challenge of serving on a submarine.

The Carters returned to their hometown of Plains, Georgia, to run the family business.

Carter thought he would stay in the navy for many years. But in 1953, his plans changed. That year, Carter's father died. At the funeral in Georgia, many people—both black and white—came to say good-bye to Earl. Carter saw that his father had been a leader in the community. He had even been elected as a state lawmaker. People respected him. Carter realized he wanted the same kind of life.

Carter shocked his wife by telling her he was quitting the navy. Instead, he wanted to return to Georgia and run his father's business. Rosalynn was not happy. She liked their life the way it was. But Carter would not take no for an answer.

The Carters stand in front of their home in Plains, Georgia.

The Carters moved to Plains, Georgia, that fall. The family included a new baby named Donnel Jeffrey. The Carters called him Jeff. Back home, Carter set a new challenge for himself. He wanted to make his father's farm and business as successful as they could be. Rosalynn was still upset about the move back to Plains. Carter thought helping out with the business would make her feel better. He was right. He and Rosalynn made a good team.

Like his father, Carter did work for his community. He volunteered to help run the local library, school, and hospital. He also remembered some of the lessons his mother had taught him.

In 1954, the country's highest court decided that segregation was against the law. But many white southerners wanted to keep schools, churches, and other places segregated anyway. Carter disagreed. He believed black people and white people should be treated equally. He lost some friends and customers because of his beliefs. But he did not change his mind.

The Carter family (FROM LEFT TO RIGHT), Chip, Jack, Rosalynn, Jimmy, and Jeff enjoy time together.

By the time Carter was thirty-seven, he had become a respected community leader. He and Rosalynn had also made their business very successful. Carter was ready for a new challenge.

One morning in 1962, he woke up and put on his best clothing. Rosalynn asked him why he was so dressed up. Carter told her he was going down to the courthouse. He wanted to sign up to run for state senate like his father had. Carter hoped to become a lawmaker for the people of Georgia.

3 LEADER IN GEORGIA

C arter and his wife worked together to help people get to know him so they would elect him to the state senate. The Carters placed an ad in the local paper. They put up posters. They made phone calls and met hundreds of people. Carter even went on the radio and TV.

Georgia state senators work at the Georgia State Capitol (LEFT) in Atlanta.

Finally, the date of the election arrived. Carter was running against a man named Homer Moore. Carter had high hopes that he could win. Then he learned some bad news. Moore was cheating. Some of his supporters had voted more than once. They voted once for themselves and again using the name of a dead person. Moore won the election.

This kind of cheating had happened in the past where Carter lived. Most people just let it go. Not Carter. He thought all elections should be fair and honest. He took his case to court. The judge had all the votes recounted. It turned out that Carter had won after all.

Carter began his state senate job in the beginning of 1963. As a state senator, he worked very hard. He became known as one of the best lawmakers in Georgia.

Three years later, he was ready for a new challenge. He decided to run for governor of Georgia, the state's highest office. Once again, the Carters worked as a team. They traveled all over the state talking to voters. Carter promised that he would make Georgia's schools, hospitals, and roads better. He said he would make the state government run better too. Carter told voters that Georgia deserved a government as good as its people.

Carter campaigns to be governor of Georgia.

Carter had grown used to meeting every challenge. He was devastated when he did not win the election. Carter talked to his sister Ruth about his disappointment. Ruth was a Christian. She told her brother to take a break from politics. She said he should focus on his religious beliefs for a while.

Carter followed his sister's advice. From then on, he made his religion an important part of his life. Carter's family life also brought him happiness. His daughter, Amy Lynn, was born in 1967.

Georgia's Capital

Atlanta is Georgia's capital city. As a lawmaker, Carter worked in Atlanta's capitol, which is the building in which the state government meets. When Carter became governor, he and his family moved to the Governor's Mansion. The Governor's Mansion in Atlanta has three floors and thirty rooms. It was a big change from the Carters' simple home in Plains.

By 1970, Carter was ready to run for governor once again. This time, he hired a team of people to help him get elected. He also met with many voters again. Some of them were white voters who wanted to keep black people and white people segregated. Some of them were black leaders in Georgia. They wanted to end segregation, which continued to exist even though it was illegal. Carter worked hard to get both sides to vote for him. In the fall of that year, Carter won the election.

Carter is sworn in as governor of Georgia.

25

On Carter's first day as governor, he gave a speech for the people of Georgia. In the speech, he said the time had come to treat the black people of Georgia as equals. His words angered some white people. Other Georgians were proud of the new governor's speech.

Another goal was to help the government spend less money. That way, Georgians could pay fewer taxes, the money that citizens and businesses pay to the government each year.

Many Georgians liked the way Governor Carter led the state. He seemed honest and hardworking. They liked the way he tried his best for the people of Georgia.

Carter (FAR RIGHT) asked many African Americans to help him run state programs.

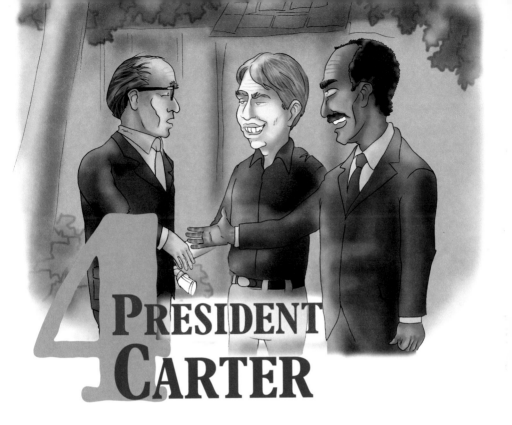

PRESIDENT CARTER

Carter liked helping to make his state's government run better. And he liked being a leader. He liked it so much that he got an idea. Maybe he could help make the U.S. government run better too.

In 1974, Carter decided to run for president of the United States. People doubted he could win the election. Most Americans had never heard of him. But he was used to working hard to meet tough challenges.

Amy, Rosalynn, and Jimmy Carter celebrate winning the Democratic nomination for president. Carter chose Walter Mondale (RIGHT) to be his running mate.

Carter would have to beat the Republican president, Gerald Ford. Carter was a member of the Democratic political party. Democrats compete in most U.S. elections with members of the Republican Party.

Carter traveled all over the United States to meet voters. He talked to newspaper, magazine, and TV reporters. He said he would be a good leader for the country. He promised that he would be fair and honest. Voters liked what they heard. Carter won the election in November 1976.

Carter had a long list of problems he hoped to solve for the country. One of his biggest goals was to save the taxpayers' money. The U.S. government spent much more money than it earned from people's taxes. That meant the government had to borrow money from other countries. So Carter found ways for the government to spend less.

Another goal was to make an energy plan. This plan would help the country save fuel, such as gasoline. To help with this work, Carter created the Department of Energy.

THE PEOPLE'S PRESIDENT

Every president begins his first day on the job with a ceremony in Washington, D.C., called an inauguration. Part of the inauguration includes a street parade from the Capitol to the White House. Presidents usually ride in a fancy car down Pennsylvania Avenue. Not Carter. Instead, he and his family walked on foot. Carter wanted people to know that he was a regular person.

Carter had many more ideas. As president, he wanted to make life better for people. He knew that millions of people in the United States were out of work. He helped to create new jobs. He also worked to make schools better. He created the Department of Education to help with that goal.

Many people liked their new president. They liked his honesty and openness. They respected his hard work for the country. But other people worried that Carter was trying to solve too many problems at once. He had so many goals, he couldn't meet them all.

President Carter meets with his cabinet at the White House. A cabinet is a group of advisers. They help the president put his ideas into action.

Carter hoped to bring peace to the world. He talked about peace with Deng Xiaoping (LEFT), the leader of China.

Carter did not stop believing in himself and his plans. Part of his plan included helping other countries. He hoped to make life better for people all over the world. He spoke out when leaders in other countries treated their citizens unfairly. He also talked about the importance of making the world a peaceful place. Two countries he worked to make peace with were China and the Soviet Union.

Carter (LEFT) shakes hands with Omar Torrijos, the leader of Panama, after signing the Panama Canal Treaties.

Carter also wanted to keep the peace with Panama and other countries in Central and South America. In the early 1900s, the United States had built the Panama Canal across Panama. This waterway created a shorter route for ships to travel from the Atlantic Ocean to the Pacific Ocean.

The United States still controlled the Panama Canal. But the people of Panama and other Latin American countries wanted that to change. Carter worried those countries might go to war with the United States. He worked with the leader of Panama to create new treaties. These agreements said that Panama would take control of the canal at the end of 1999.

Carter also worried about the wars happening in Arab countries of the Middle East. Countries in the Middle East are located in southwest Asia and northeast Africa. The fighting was taking place between Israel and Arab countries.

In 1948, the state of Israel was created for the Jewish people. But Israel's Arab neighbors, such as Egypt, believed that Israel belonged to a group of Arab people called the Palestinians. The leader of Egypt, Anwar Sadat, wanted to make peace with Israel. He hoped to set an example for other Arab leaders. But he needed help.

Carter (RIGHT) and Anwar Sadat (LEFT), the leader of Egypt, hoped to bring peace to the Middle East.

In September 1978, Carter invited Israel's leader, Menachem Begin, and Anwar Sadat to the United States. They met at Camp David in Maryland. This quiet place was created for U.S. presidents to visit when they needed to relax.

Carter met with the two leaders together and apart. He worked hard to earn their trust. But the two leaders did not trust each other. At times, Sadat and Begin wanted to give up. But Carter wouldn't let them. He found ways for both sides to compromise. After thirteen days, the two leaders agreed on a plan for a peace treaty. This was called the Camp David Accords.

The leaders of Egypt and Israel sign the peace treaty.

Iranians hung anti-American posters on the U.S. Embassy in Iran. Inside, terrorists held American hostages.

Carter faced another problem in 1979. That year, the leader of Iran was forced to give up his power. A new leader took over. Carter allowed Iran's old leader to seek safety and treatment for an illness in the United States. That made many people in Iran angry.

On November 4, Iranian terrorists took over the U.S. Embassy in Iran. An embassy is a place in another country where government representatives live and work. The terrorists held more than fifty Americans hostage. Carter worked hard to bring the hostages home to the United States. But the terrorists refused to give them up.

In 1980, Carter ran for reelection. He had to beat the Republican candidate, Ronald Reagan. Many voters wanted a new leader. They thought that Carter could not solve the country's biggest problems.

Carter lost the election that fall. But he still had two more months as president. During that time, he worked as hard as he could to save the hostages in Iran. But he could not convince the terrorists to free them. Finally, after 444 days, the hostages were freed just a few minutes after Carter's presidency ended.

Carter lost the presidential election in 1980 to Ronald Reagan (LEFT).

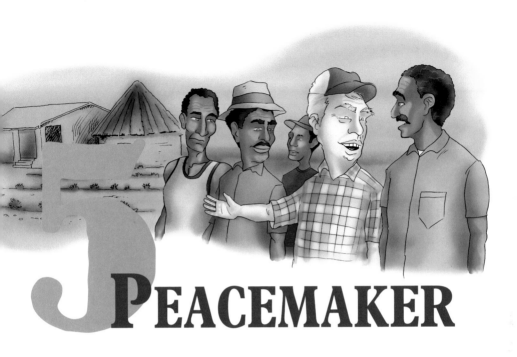

5 PEACEMAKER

Carter and his family returned to their home in Plains, Georgia, in January 1981. Carter was fifty-six years old. He had many years ahead of him. But he had no idea what to do next. Without his job as president, he felt lost.

An idea came to Carter one winter morning in 1982. Why not continue his work as a peacemaker? Perhaps he could open up a place where leaders could work out their disagreements. He would call it the Carter Center.

In 1986, the Carter Center in Atlanta, Georgia, officially began its important work to promote peace. Carter asked his wife to help run it. Their adult children also volunteered to help.

Carter and other workers at the center organized meetings about making peace. Leaders from many countries came to the meetings.

The Carters celebrate the opening of the Carter Center.

Carter shakes hands with Shimon Peres, an Israeli politician. Carter was in Israel to promote peace.

Carter hoped these leaders would use the ideas they had learned there. Then they could help to keep major wars that involved many nations from happening.

Carter knew that many countries also suffered from wars that were fought among people in the same country. The fighting killed thousands of men, women, and children each year. The Carter Center began keeping track of these wars. Carter began to travel to many of these countries to try to bring about peace.

Carter (LEFT) *oversaw the 1996 Palestinian election. Yasser Arafat* (RIGHT) *won the election.*

In the late 1980s, Carter found another way for the Carter Center to help. Many countries in Africa, Latin America, Asia, and other places were having democratic elections for the first time. Sometimes the leaders of these countries cheated to stay in power. Over the years, Carter has traveled to many countries during elections. He helped to make sure that the elections were fair.

With the Carter Center, Carter also works to keep people healthy. He and others have helped protect people in poor countries from deadly diseases. Workers from the Carter Center have also helped farmers in Africa grow more food. That way, people in those countries will have more to eat.

A GREAT HONOR

Carter's hard work and determination has inspired many people. In 2002, he received the Nobel Peace Prize. This award is one of the most respected honors in the world. It is given out only once each year. It has honored some of the world's greatest peacemakers.

Carter's life is busy. But he still finds time to have fun. One of his favorite hobbies is fly-fishing. Another hobby is carpentry. At home, he enjoys making furniture from wood.

Since 1984, Carter has used his skills as a carpenter to help others. Each year, he and Rosalynn spend a week volunteering with Habitat for Humanity. This organization builds houses for people who do not have a place to live. The Carters have helped build homes in the United States and many other countries.

The Carters build a house for Habitat for Humanity in Atlanta, Georgia.

Carter speaks with a woman in Liberia. He was there with the Carter Center to monitor the 2005 elections.

Over the years, Carter has helped people in more than sixty-five nations. And he is always ready to do more. He has worked hard for his country and for people around the world. His hard work inspires others to make a difference.

TIMELINE

In the year . . .

1928   Jimmy's family moved to Archery, Georgia.   Age 3

1941   he graduated from high school.
       he went to Georgia Southwestern College.

1942   he went to Georgia Tech for a year.

1943   he went to study at the U.S. Naval Academy.

1946   he graduated from the Naval Academy.   Age 21
       he married Rosalynn Smith on July 7.

1947   his first son, John William, was born.

1949   Jimmy and his family moved to Hawaii.

1950   his second son, James Earl III, was born.

1952   Jimmy's third son, Donnel Jeffrey, was born.

1953   Jimmy left the navy and moved with his
       family back to Plains, Georgia.

1962   he ran for state senator and won.   Age 38

1966   he lost an election for governor of Georgia.

1967   his daughter, Amy Lynn, was born.

1970   he ran for governor a second time and won.

1976   he won the election for president.   Age 52

1977   he created the Department of Energy.

1978   the Camp David talks took place.

1979   the Department of Education was created.

1980   he lost reelection as president.

1982   he established the Carter Center.   Age 58

1999   he was awarded the Presidential Medal of
       Freedom.

2002   he won the Nobel Peace Prize.   Age 78

2005   he spoke at a ceremony for a U.S. Navy
       submarine that was named for him.

ROSALYNN CARTER:
A GREAT AMERICAN WOMAN

In her lifetime, Rosalynn has been part of a strong team with her husband. But she has also worked hard on her own goals. For many years, Rosalynn has spoken out for people with mental illnesses. A mental illness is a disease of the mind. It can harm a person's mood, thoughts, and behavior.

People with mental illnesses have not always been treated fairly in the United States. Rosalynn has fought hard to change that. She has helped to get new laws passed that have made life better for mentally ill citizens.

Rosalynn has also spoken out for the rights of women. She has worked to make sure that poor children have better health care. And she has fought for the fair treatment of people around the world. Rosalynn has been given many awards and honors for her work. In 2001, she was voted into the National Women's Hall of Fame. The Hall of Fame in Seneca Falls, New York, honors great American women. Rosalynn has inspired many people. Like Jimmy, she is helping to make the world a better place.

Rosalynn receives a Caring for Children lifetime achievement award in 2002.

FURTHER READING

Keene, Ann T. *Peacemakers: Winners of the Nobel Peace Prize.* New York: Oxford University Press, 1998. Provides summaries on the lives and achievements of all the winners of the Nobel Peace Prize.

Kent, Deborah. *Jimmy Carter: America's 39th President.* Danbury, CT: Children's Press, 2005. This biography reviews the life and career of U.S. president Jimmy Carter.

Kramer, Barbara. *Jimmy Carter: A Life of Service.* Berkeley Heights, NJ: Enslow, 2005. This biography provides more information on U.S. president Jimmy Carter.

Turk, Ruth. *Rosalynn Carter: Steel Magnolia.* Danbury, CT: Franklin Watts, 1997. Reviews the life and career of Rosalynn Carter, former First Lady of the United States.

WEBSITES

American Experience: Jimmy Carter
http://www.pbs.org/wgbh/amex/carter/ View images and learn more about Jimmy Carter's life and career.

Biography of Jimmy Carter
http://www.whitehouse.gov/history/presidents/jc39.html Read about Jimmy Carter on the White House website.

The Carter Center
http://www.cartercenter.org/ Read about the history and activities of the Carter Center on its official website.

Jimmy Carter and Habitat for Humanity
http://www.habitat.org/how/carter.aspx/ Read about Jimmy Carter's work with Habitat for Humanity.

SELECT BIBLIOGRAPHY

BOOKS
Bourne, Peter G. *Jimmy Carter: A Comprehensive Biography.* New York: Scribner, 1997.

Brinkley, Douglas. *An Unfinished Presidency: Jimmy Carter's Journey beyond the White House.* New York: Viking, 1998.

Carter, Jimmy. *An Hour before Daylight: Memories of a Rural Boyhood.* New York: Simon and Schuster, 2001.

Carter, Jimmy. *Keeping Faith: Memoirs of a President.* New York: Bantam Books, 1982.

Carter, Jimmy. *Sharing Good Times.* New York: Simon and Schuster, 2004.

Carter, Jimmy. *Turning Point: A Candidate, a State, and a Nation Come of Age.* New York: Times Books, 1992.

Carter, Jimmy, and Rosalynn Carter. *Everything to Gain: Making the Most of the Rest of Your Life.* New York: Random House, 1987.

Morris, Kenneth E. *Jimmy Carter: American Moralist.* Athens: University of Georgia Press, 1996.

VIDEO
Jimmy Carter. Boston: PBS Home Video, WGBH, 2002.

INDEX

Atlanta, Georgia, 22, 24, 38

Begin, Menachem, 34

Camp David Accords, 34
Carter, Jimmy: birth of, 6;
childhood of, 6–12; children
of, 14, 16, 18, 24; education
of, 13; father of, 6–8, 17; as
governor, 25–27; marriage
of, 14; mother of, 9; as
president, 28–36; as senator,
22–23; sisters of, 6, 24
Carter, Rosalynn Smith
(wife), 13, 14, 16, 42
Carter Center, 38–41

Democratic political party, 28
Department of Education, 30
Department of Energy, 29

Ford, Gerald, 28

Habitat for Humanity, 42

inauguration, 29

Middle East, 33

Nobel Peace Prize, 41

Panama Canal, 32

Reagan, Ronald, 36
Republican Party, 28

Sadat, Anwar, 33–34
segregation, 11, 19
sharecroppers, 10
Smith, Rosalynn. See Carter,
Rosalynn Smith (wife)

United States Naval
Academy, 12–13, 14

Acknowledgments

The images in this book are used with the permission of: Jimmy Carter Library,
pp. 4, 8, 9, 10, 11, 12, 13, 18, 23, 25, 30, 32, 34; © CORBIS, p. 7; Naval Historical
Center (80-G-1042402), p. 15; Library of Congress, pp. 16 (LC-USZ-62-70726), 33
(LC-DIG-ppmsca-09815); © Kevin Fleming/CORBIS, p. 17; © Bettmann/CORBIS,
pp. 19, 31, 38, 42; © W. Cody/CORBIS, p. 22; Boyd Lewis/Atlanta Historical
Society, p. 26; © Hulton Archive/Getty Images, p. 28; © STAFF/AFP/Getty
Images, p. 35; Courtesy Ronald Reagan Library, p. 36; © SVEN
NACKSTRAND/AFP/Getty Images, p. 39; © GILBERT LIZ/CORBIS SYGMA, p.
40; © Arne Knudsen/Getty Images, p. 41; © Chris Hondros/Getty Images, p. 43;
AP/Wide World Photos, p. 45.

Front Cover: © PAUL J. RICHARDS/AFP/Getty Images
Back Cover: © Bettmann/CORBIS

True or False?

Jimmy Carter is often known as America's best ex-president.

True! In the years since he left office in 1981, Carter has been involved in many political and charitable causes.

- He founded the Carter Center, which works to fight disease and bring peace to countries at war.

- He works with Habitat for Humanity to build houses for people who do not have a place to live.

- He was awarded the Presidential Medal of Freedom in 1999 and the Nobel Peace Prize in 2002.

Read these other History Maker Bios

PRESIDENTS AND PATRIOTS OF OUR COUNTRY

Abigail Adams • John Adams • Susan B. Anthony
Dwight D. Eisenhower • Benjamin Franklin • John Hancock
Patrick Henry • Andrew Jackson • Thomas Jefferson • John F. Kennedy
Abraham Lincoln • Dolley Madison • Paul Revere • Franklin D. Roosevelt
Theodore Roosevelt • George Washington • Woodrow Wilson

BARNES & NOBLE
NEW YORK

U.S. $5.95 /Canada $7.95
ISBN-13: 978-0-7607-7507-3
ISBN-10: 0-7607-7507-9

50595

9 780760 775073